SOUNDBITES

Percussion

Roger Thomas

Heinemann Library
Chicago, Illinois

Designed by Paul Davies and Associates
Originated by Ambassador Litho Ltd.
Printed at Wing King Tong in Hong Kong

06 05 04 03 02
10 9 8 7 6 5 4 3 2 1

Library of Congress Cataloging-in-Publication Data
Thomas, Roger, 1956-
  Percussion / Roger Thomas.
      p. cm. -- (Soundbites)
Includes bibliographical references (p.   ) and index.
  ISBN 1-58810-265-3
  1. Percussion instruments--Juvenile literature. [1. Percussion
instruments.] I. Title. II. Series.
  ML1030 .T48 2001
  786.8'19--dc21
                                2001001725

Acknowledgments
The author and publishers are grateful to the following for permission to reproduce copyright material:
Cover photograph: Chris Honeywell.
pp. 4, 13, 21 Jazz Index; pp. 5, 25 Christian Him; pp. 6, 7, 9 Trevor Clifford; p. 6 Liz Eddison; pp. 6, 14, 15 Eyewire; p. 6 Chris Howes; pp. 8, 10, 12, 16, 17, 22, 24 Lebrecht Picture Library; p. 11 Corbis; pp. 18, 19, 26, 27, 28 Redferns; p. 20 South American Photos; p. 23 Powerstock Zefa; p. 29 Dat's Jazz Picture Library.

Special thanks to Dane Richeson for his comments in the preparation of this book.

Every effort has been made to contact copyright holders of any material reproduced in this book. Any omissions will be rectified in subsequent printings if notice is given to the publisher.

Some words are shown in bold, **like this.** You can find out what they mean by looking in the glossary.

Contents

Introduction

Percussion instruments were probably the first musical instruments of all, after the human voice. All percussion instruments produce sound in the simplest way possible—by the impact of one object against another, or in some cases by **friction.** Percussion is also strongly associated with **rhythm,** as in the basic patterns central to human life—for example, the rhythms of heartbeats, breathing, walking, running, and chewing food. Some musicians today feel that percussion should not really be thought of as a group of instruments, but as a way of playing. This is partly because the percussion family is so varied, but also because most other types of instruments can also be played using percussive techniques, such as playing bowed stringed instruments *col legno* (tapping the strings with the wooden part of the bow) or rattling the keys of a woodwind instrument (sometimes required in **avant-garde** music).

An extraordinary history

There is no musical culture anywhere in the world that does not have a tradition of making and playing percussion instruments. Virtually every form of classical, popular, and folk music in every country involves this family of instruments in some way. Percussion instruments are used in many musical contexts, as listed on page five.

Timpani drums are played in a classical orchestra.

- Classical Music: Most larger orchestras include a percussion section; these can vary in size.
- Band and Ensemble Music: Different types of percussion instruments are used in marching bands and **chamber groups.** There are even percussion **ensembles,** where all the instruments used are some form of tuned or untuned percussion.
- Pop Music: The drum set began as a theater instrument, but it has long since become central to both the sound and image of popular music. Other forms of percussion are also widely used in popular music. These range from Latin and African drums, such as congas, djembes, and timbales, that may also be used in rock music, to tuned percussion, such as the vibraphone.

The drum set is an instantly recognizable icon of the percussion world.

- Folk and World Music: While it is misleading to describe the rest of the world's musical traditions as if they somehow made up a single vast musical **genre,** it is perhaps the only convenient way to begin to examine the huge variety of percussion instruments used in different cultures worldwide. However, it is interesting to note how many similar designs of percussion instruments, such as drums, exist all over the world. In that sense, the percussion traditions of different cultures do have a great deal in common.

Types of Percussion Instruments

All percussion instruments rely on one object making contact with another in order to produce sound. However, even this is not an ideal definition, as it is also true of many other instruments. A guitar relies on the player's fingers or a **pick** plucking the strings to make a sound. The action of plucking is not normally associated with percussion, but if an electric guitarist plays by "hammering" the strings against the **frets** with his or her fingertips without plucking the strings, does this somehow transform the guitar into a percussion instrument?

Musicologists have traditionally avoided getting sidetracked into arguments of this kind by using a very precise set of terms to describe how different instruments make sounds. These terms were devised in 1914 by two musicologists, Erich von Hornbostel and Curt Sachs, and have been in use ever since. They deal with every type of instrument, but there are two main categories for percussion instruments.

One group, **membranophones,** are instruments that rely on an attached vibrating **membrane** to make a sound. This class includes drums of all types.

Idiophones, on the other hand, are instruments made of materials that produce their sounds directly, without a membrane. This definition effectively covers every type of percussion instrument other than drums, including cymbals, bells, gongs, rattles and shakers, wood blocks, and tuned percussion such as the xylophone. Within this category, the instruments are then classified

The instruments shown on this page are membranophones.

according to exactly how the player has to use the instrument to produce a sound, with further subgroups that describe what the instrument is made of. For example, marimbas and glockenspiels are grouped together because they are both tuned percussion instruments played in a similar way. However, this category can still be subdivided, because the bars of a marimba are made of wood, whereas the bars of a glockenspiel are made of metal.

A matter of definition

Despite this careful distinction, there are still gray areas. For example, log drums, made from hollowed-out trees, are played by beating and can sound much like drums. However, because they have no membranes, log drums are not really drums at all and are therefore not classed as membranophones.

The instruments above are very different in sound and appearance, but they are all idiophones.

The cajón

The cajón, played in Cuba and South America, is a percussion instrument that looks like a wooden box. It has one thin playing surface that is slapped with the hands. Is this a wooden "membrane"? Or is the cajón an idiophone? Sometimes there is no right answer.

The Parts of Percussion Instruments

Percussion covers many different types of instruments, and any single type of instrument can be designed in a variety of ways. However, all percussion instruments have three important parts that can be identified on any instrument in the percussion family.

Three basic elements

Every percussion instrument has a surface for striking, a part or area that makes the sound **audible** (or "shapes" the sound in the desired way), and one or more parts that allow the sound of the instrument to be changed in some way. Sometimes one part will have two or all three functions, as you will see below.

On a drum, for example, the surface to be struck is the drumhead, or simply, the **head.** While this itself makes an audible noise, the shell of the drum gives the sound a **resonant tone.** The sound on many drums can be changed by raising the **pitch** of the drumhead using a **tensioning** mechanism. Modern **Western** drums use a series of screw bolts, called tension rods, that fit through holes on a rim that is placed over the edge of the drum's head. The tension rods are screwed into metal blocks, called lugs, that are fixed to the shell. These rods are then tightened, raising the tension of the drumhead.

There are three important parts of a marimba: the bars, resonators, and supporting frame.

On a marimba, the surface to be struck is a set of wooden bars. Because the marimba is a tuned percussion instrument, the sound is changed simply by striking different bars. This sound is audible as it is, but it is **amplified** by a set of tube-shaped **resonators** that hang underneath the instrument.

On a cymbal or tam-tam, the striking surface, the area that makes the sound audible, and the area that can be used to change the sound—for example, by **damping, choking,** or adding **sizzlers**—are one and the same.

On a maraca, the striking surface is the inside of the instrument. The hollow area inside the instrument makes the sound more audible. The sound is altered by varying the speed, direction, and amount of force used in shaking the instrument. So the mechanism for changing the sound is, essentially, the handle!

Can you identify the important parts of these instruments?

Sticks and beaters

Some instruments may seem to be missing one of these three elements, but a bit of careful thinking will show that they are always present, even in the design of a very simple instrument, such as a wood block. It has a striking surface and a hollowed-out area that creates a sharp, distinct sound. However, how can the sound be changed? The answer is that all percussion instruments require the use of an object to strike them—a stick or beater, the human hand, or, in the case of bells and shakers, something contained within the instrument—and these are really parts of the instruments themselves. In the case of a wood block, the sound is changed simply by using a softer or harder beater. This applies to many other percussion instruments, too.

Orchestral and Band Drums

The various specialized drums that are found in **Western** orchestral and marching band music are quite similar in many ways. This is because both ranges of drums evolved from various earlier military drums.

Standard orchestral drums

Although many types of drums can be included in the percussion sections of Western orchestras, some are specifically associated with this type of music. One example, the **snare** drum, is a **double-headed** drum with a set of wires stretched across the bottom **head** that produces a buzzing sound when the drum is struck. Drums of this type are also used in popular and marching band music. The orchestral snare drum is of a particular design that is deeper than a rock or jazz snare drum, but shallower than a marching band snare drum. It is sometimes referred to as a "side drum" because of the playing position of the military drum from which it was developed. Its relative, the **tenor** drum, is also double-headed, but it is deeper than the snare drum and has no snare wires. It has a dark, booming **tone.**

The timpani are just one of the types of drums used in orchestral music.

The **bass** drum is a very large, double-headed drum that can produce a range of sounds from a muffled rumble to a thunderous crack depending on how hard it is struck. The orchestral bass drum is much bigger than the bass drums used as a part of rock and jazz drum sets.

The timpani, sometimes called kettledrums, are perhaps the drums most associated with classical music. They were developed from military drums that were played on horseback. They are very large drums, each with a single head stretched over a metal bowl. Modern timpani can be tuned to a range of notes by using pedals that change the **tension** of the head.

Marching band drums

Marching bands use some of the same kinds of drums as in orchestras, but there are some differences. For example, the snare drum used in marching bands is larger and louder than that used in orchestral music. The player "wears" the drum, either in front of the body or at a slight angle to allow the player to march. This position means that the player may have to hold the two drumsticks in slightly different ways in order to play the drum comfortably. This same technique, traditionally taught to drum students, is also used by many classical and jazz players, as well as some rock players.

The bass drum played by marching band drummers is strapped to the player's chest and is struck on both sides. In American marching bands, there are often several bass drums that are tuned to different **pitches.**

Marching toms are related to concert toms. These **single-headed, melodic** drums are strapped in front of the player. They usually come as a set of several drums of different sizes. Many have angled openings at the bottom of each drum, that encourage the sound to project outward rather than downward.

Marching toms are uniquely designed for use in marching bands.

Cymbals, Gongs, and Bells

These three types of instruments are related, although they actually evolved in very different ways.

Cymbals

Cymbals are used in all kinds of music throughout the world. These instruments have probably been in use for around 3,000 years, and some evidence suggests that they may have evolved from metal drinking bowls. One well-known example of ancient cymbals was the pair of instruments that were found buried with the

Cymbals are made in a wide range of sizes and thicknesses.

mummified body of the musician Ankhape, who lived in ancient Egypt during the first century B.C.E. However, the two most important cymbal-making traditions evolved in China and Turkey. Virtually all modern cymbals are based on these designs, though the two types are quite different in sound and appearance. Cymbals are generally made of bronze, a mixture of copper and tin. However, other metals can be used, including brass (a mixture of copper and zinc) or a mixture of nickel and silver.

A cymbal is essentially a metal disk with a slight downward curve toward the edge. It usually has an upward-curved bell shape in the center, although a few designs do not have this. Chinese cymbals also have an upturned area around the edge. There is a hole in the center that allows the cymbal to be hung on a stand or attached to a handle. Cymbals can be played in two ways: they can be struck with a stick or beater, or two cymbals can be clashed together. Different sizes and thicknesses of cymbals produce a variety of sounds. In classical and popular music, cymbals may be played on stands. Classical players will also use a pair of matched cymbals with strap handles to clash together. Marching band players may use a pair of cymbals in this way, too. A similar effect is produced by an instrument called a hi-hat, which is used in popular music, with two cymbals on a stand attached to a pedal. The cymbals are clashed together when the pedal is pressed.

Gongs

This type of gong is from Malaysia.

Gongs differ from cymbals in that they have no central hole, but are instead suspended from one edge. They are almost always made of bronze and come in a wide range of sizes. The gongs most widely used today are Chinese in origin. Unlike the crash produced by cymbals, gongs have a subtler, richer sound. They are often referred to by their Chinese names, like the tam-tam and wind gong, that produces a sustained hissing sound. Gongs are often used in classical music, occasionally in rock, and, of course, in traditional Chinese music.

Bells

Bells are usually cup-shaped metal instruments. A bell may have a suspended internal hammer called a clapper that hits against the inside of the bell to make the sound. Bells are found in many cultures and may be as small as a pea (tiny Indian bells known as "cat bells") or as large as a house! They are one of the most widely known types of percussion instruments.

Wood Blocks, Cowbells, and Hand Percussion

These instruments are quite diverse in terms of how they are made and played. However, they are often found together in certain forms of music, such as classical, Latin American, and folk music, so it can be useful to be able to distinguish them from one another.

Wood blocks

Wood blocks are made of hard wood. There are several different types, but two varieties are most commonly used. One, the basic wood block, is shaped like an oblong box with one or more slits cut along its length. It is made in several different sizes, may be mounted on a clamp, and is played with a stick or beater. It produces a crisp, hard "clack" sound.

Another type of wood block, temple blocks, also come in various sizes and are often played on a stand in tuned sets. Of Chinese origin, the traditional design is made from camphor wood and is more or less **spherical** in shape, with a hollowed-out interior (this design led to their being nicknamed "skulls" at one time). There are also **Western** designs that are more cube-shaped.

Cowbells

As the name implies, these are similar to the traditional metal bells tied around the necks of cattle. There are several different kinds, including **chromatically** tuned sets of cowbells that are usually played by classical percussionists, particularly when playing in percussion **ensemble** pieces. These are very similar in shape to traditional cattle bells. In Latin American music on the other hand, cowbells come in several sizes and are usually shaped like metal boxes, narrower at one end than the other. The sound comes out through the open, wider end. The narrow end is closed and may have a hole or fitting for mounting the instrument on a stand. Some types have no holes and are simply held in the hand, while others have handles. A hammer handle is sometimes used as a beater for handheld cowbells.

Auxiliary percussion

The phrase "auxiliary percussion," or hand percussion, is used by percussionists to describe any small instrument that is held in the hand. Some examples of these include the following:

- The tambourine is a circular frame with metal jingles attached. Some types also have a **head** attached, like a frame drum.
- Maracas are traditional Latin American shakers made from hard leather, wood, metal, or plastic and filled with hard pellets or seeds. There are many other types of shakers as well, like the tube-shaped chocolo.
- Sleigh bells are a set of small jingling bells attached to a handle; they are widely used in Christmas music.

Tuned Percussion

While many kinds of percussion can be tuned to an extent—for example, the **pitches** of a set of drums can be adjusted to produce a range of notes—the phrase "tuned percussion" is usually used to describe **melodic** percussion instruments that play specific notes like a piano. These instruments are often laid out in a similar way to a piano keyboard. They usually consist of a set of bars for striking and often have tubes suspended beneath the bars to **amplify** the sound of the bars. They are usually used in classical music, but some similar instruments are used in marching bands.

The glockenspiel (German for "playable bells") is a set of high-pitched metal bars that have a distinctive, bright sound. There are also glockenspiels that have a keyboard mechanism—one example is the **celeste,** used in the famous "Dance of the Sugar-Plum Fairy" by Russian composer Pyotr Tchaikovsky (1840–93). Yet another version is mounted on a portable frame for use by marching bands. This type is usually known as **lyre** bells, because the frame looks similar to the frame of a stringed instrument called a lyre.

The xylophone has wooden bars that give a distinctive "plink" sound when struck with a hard beater. Its relative, the marimba, is essentially a **bass** xylophone. It plays lower notes and has a warmer, more **resonant tone** than the xylophone. There is also

The playing technique shown here can be applied to many tuned percussion instruments.

an old instrument, called a xylorimba, that can cover the range of the xylophone plus part of the range of the marimba.

The vibraphone is normally associated with jazz, but it is also used in some classical pieces, such as the opera *Lulu* by Austrian composer Alban Berg (1885–1935). It has metal bars and **resonating** tubes that have small, motor-driven fans at the top. These rotate slowly, adding a shimmering **tremolo** effect to the sound of the bars. Soft beaters are usually used to play the vibraphone.

The tubaphone is more unusual and consists of a set of tuned metal tubes instead of bars. Like the glockenspiel, there are versions designed both for orchestras and for marching bands.

Another instrument with tubes, the tubular bells, are sometimes known as orchestral chimes. These large, vertical, tube-shaped bells are suspended on a vertical frame and struck near the top with mallets.

The tubular bells are one kind of tuned percussion instrument.

Electronic and digital tuned percussion

These more modern types of instruments are laid out like other tuned percussion instruments, but each "bar" consists of a rubbery surface with an electronic sensor underneath. When struck, these bars transmit an electronic signal that the player can adjust in many different ways. This allows the instrument to produce **synthesized** and **sampled** sounds.

Jazz and Rock Drums

The drum set is one of the most easily recognizable instrument sets in music. Its use began in the theater at a time when theater bands and orchestras used a set of percussion instruments broadly similar to those used in the symphony orchestra, including a **snare** drum and a **bass** drum. However, the restricted space available in smaller theaters (together with an unwillingness on the part of bandleaders to employ more than one percussionist) would often mean that a single player would play both snare and bass drums. This led to the invention of the bass drum pedal, a device with a beater attached to a hinged footplate that remains central to the functioning of the drum set today. This pedal made the whole task much easier by allowing the player to use both hands to play the snare drum or other instruments.

A typical drum set

Both jazz and rock drum sets are similar in that each will generally consist of a bass drum, a snare drum, and two or more tom-toms (snareless drums of varying sizes and **pitches**). Some rock drummers like to use two bass drums, a larger number of tom-toms, and even a second, higher-pitched snare drum. The basic set also includes a number of cymbals, some of which are designed for playing with single, hard strokes ("crash" cymbals), while others are tapped rhythmically in time with the music ("ride" cymbals). Most sets also use a hi-hat, that allows two cymbals to be clashed together with a pedal. The drums and cymbals are

This is a typical jazz drum set. It includes a bass drum, a snare drum, tom-toms, and cymbals.

played with sticks, brushes (bundles of wire or plastic filaments attached to a handle), or sometimes, for special effects, soft beaters. Some drummers may add other percussion instruments such as cowbells or wood blocks. Today, the primary difference between jazz and rock drum sets is size. Jazz music tends to demand subtler drum sounds and is often played in smaller venues, so jazz drum sets are often smaller.

Rock drummers tend to use larger drum kits.

Jazz drums

The use of drum sets in jazz and popular dance music is virtually as old as the music itself. Early jazz drum sets were often assembled from a variety of different sources, including marching band and military instruments. One important innovation was the development of various devices that allowed the player to clash two cymbals together with a pedal. Together with the bass drum pedal, this enabled the drummer to play both the "onbeat" (ONE-two-THREE-four) and the "offbeat" (one-TWO-three-FOUR) without using hands at all. The modern hi-hat evolved from these earlier inventions.

Rock drums

The growth of rock music placed many new demands on drum sets. Because of the use of **amplified** instruments and the fact that the music was originally intended to be heard and recognized on the radio, rock music tended to be louder than jazz from the beginning. This meant that rock drums, cymbals, and stands all became larger, heavier, and stronger as the music **genre** developed.

Latin and African Percussion

The tradition of drumming and percussion playing in Latin and African cultures is very old. It still continues to develop, while the playing styles associated with the music of these cultures have influenced the rock, pop, and jazz music of North America and Europe in many different ways.

Afro/Latin percussion instruments come in many sizes and shapes.

Latin instruments

The **rhythms** of Latin and Afro-Cuban music are associated with very specific instruments. One kind, congas, are drums that are usually shaped like elongated barrels (traditional congas were in fact made from recycled rum barrel **staves**). Some examples may also have a **tapered,** cylindrical shape. A conga has a single **head** that is played with the hands. Congas can be played singly or in sets of two or more different sizes.

Another type, bongos, are smaller drums of two different sizes. They are usually played as a pair tuned approximately an **octave** apart. Bongos are traditionally held between the player's knees, although more recent bongos have become larger and are often played on a stand, with the player standing or sitting behind them.

Timbales are **single-headed** drums with metal shells. They are played with sticks, with the player using both the heads and shells of the drums as striking surfaces.

Small percussion instruments used in Latin music include cowbells and maracas. Other types include the guiro, a ridged tube made from dried **gourd,** metal, wood, or **fiberglass** and played with a scraper; and claves, a kind of short, smooth wooden sticks that are clicked together, with the player using the cupped palm of one hand as a **resonator.**

African instruments

An enormous variety of percussion instruments are used in African music as well. Interestingly, versions of many of these traditional instruments are now made by **Western** manufacturers using **synthetic** materials.

The djembe is a distinctive single-headed drum with an hourglass shape, that comes in many sizes. It is played with the hands and produces a specific range of sounds, from high-**pitched** overtones to deep, booming notes that are made by forcing air through the drum's narrow "waist" by slapping the head hard in the center.

The talking drum is also shaped like an hourglass, but it has two heads that are joined together loosely with thin leather **thongs.** It is tucked under the player's arm and is traditionally played with a hand and one stick. When the player squeezes the thongs, the drumheads are tightened, raising the pitch of the drum.

The balafon is a type of African xylophone made from wooden bars, with dried gourds underneath that act as resonators.

Middle Eastern and Far Eastern Percussion

Middle Eastern percussion instruments

There are several instruments that are used, with some variations in design and name, in many Middle Eastern and North African countries. Some are also found in nearby parts of Asia and Europe.

The dhumbek, or darabouka, is a **single-headed** drum with an hourglass shape. It is found in several areas, including Turkey and Middle Eastern countries. The shell is usually made of metal or pottery. The dhumbek gets its name from the extremely wide range of **tones** it can produce, from very low (sounding like "dhum") to very high (sounding like "BEK!"). The low notes are made by slapping the drumhead hard in the center, forcing air through the narrow "waist" of the drum, as with the African djembe.

The tar is an Arab frame drum with a **head** made from stretched goatskin. Like other frame drums, it has a very shallow shell that acts as a frame for stretching the drumhead rather than acting as a **resonator.** It is played with the hands and fingertips and has a remarkably delicate and **resonant** sound.

The riq is the Egyptian equivalent of the tambourine. It is a shallow, round frame drum with a goatskin head and several sets of jingles.

The dhumbek, or darabouka, is widely used in Middle Eastern music.

Far Eastern percussion

Many percussion instruments in China and Japan often have religious uses. (As do percussion instruments from other cultures.) One example, taiko drums, are traditional Japanese drums used in playing *kagura* music, meaning "God music." New *kagura* music is still being written today, and there are several famous groups of taiko drummers that tour other countries to perform.

Japanese taiko drums can reach immense sizes!

"Chinese tom-toms" is the English name given to traditional Chinese drums with wood shells and two heads made from pigskin. Although mainly associated with Chinese classical music, these were also used in the **West** as parts of the first drum kits, when they were often played to produce "jungle" sound effects. They are traditionally painted with a bright red lacquer and have metal rings attached to the shells that allow them to be suspended from stands. While the very largest examples produce a deep booming sound, the smaller, shallower sizes produce a gentle, delicate tone, particularly if they are played with soft beaters.

Cup gongs are found in both Japan and China. They are simple looking bronze bowls that are made in many different sizes. They are rested, open end up, on a cushioned support and played gently with a wooden beater covered in soft leather. They have a complex yet delicate tone.

Other gongs, cymbals, and bells are also important in most forms of Far Eastern music, from popular entertainment to religious music. For example, large gongs can be found hanging in Japanese religious shrines. In Chinese opera, two cymbals may be clashed together to emphasize dramatic situations.

Indonesian, Indian, and Australian Percussion

Many percussion instruments have evolved in the musical cultures of Java, Bali, India, Australia, and other countries in this region. Despite—or perhaps because of—the fact that many of these instruments sound nothing like **Western** percussion instruments, their unique sounds have attracted audiences and enthusiasts worldwide.

Javanese and Balinese percussion

The gamelan orchestra is a traditional percussion **ensemble** found in Java and Bali. The orchestra uses a range of gongs and tuned metal percussion instruments to produce a highly disciplined form of **rhythmic** music consisting of complex sequences of bell-like **tones.** The instruments can include individual gongs like the ageng and suwukan, with low and high **pitch,** respectively; multiple-gong instruments like the bonang barung and kengong; and other types of tuned percussion made with bronze bars and played with wooden beaters and hammers, including the saron, slentem, gender, and gangsa. The orchestra also includes various drums, cymbals, and xylophones.

The gamelan orchestra has a distinctive and fascinating sound.

Indian percussion

The tabla are hand drums with an immediately recognizable sound. A set consists of two different drums. One is usually made of wood and is roughly cylindrical in shape, with a high pitch. The other is basin-shaped and usually made of metal, with a low pitch. Both are **single-headed** drums with closed ends. The **heads** have black circles on them, made from a sticky paste that, when dry, improves the sound of the drums. The drums are played with a variety of complex hand and finger strokes, with the player varying the pitch of the lower drum by pressing on the head while playing. Each type of stroke has a name and the process of saying these names aloud has evolved into a musical art in its own right—a kind of "vocal percussion."

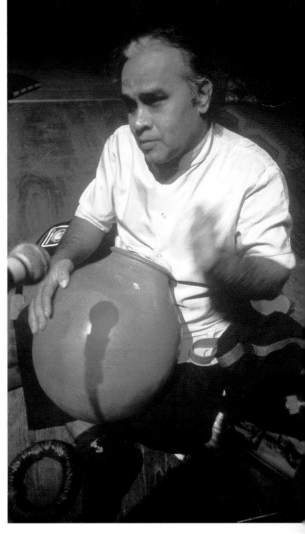

The ghatam is a clever and unusual instrument—essentially it is a large clay pot with a single hole that is pressed against the player's stomach. The player slaps the ghatam with the left hand to produce low notes, while producing higher notes with the fingers and nails of the other hand. By moving the hole closer to and away from the body, the player can produce a variety of tones. Indian musicians often say that a large stomach is an advantage for a ghatam player!

The ghatam can be played both on its own or as part of a musical group.

Aboriginal Australian percussion

Clappers, percussion sticks that are struck together (such as claves), and stamping sticks that are beaten upon the ground are among the percussion instruments used by Aboriginal Australians. As with the percussion instruments found in many other cultures, their use is often strongly associated with religion and ritual.

Percussion Recording and Performance Technology

Anyone who has heard a drummer practicing may wonder why microphones ever need to be used for percussion instruments at all! However, the fact is that microphones have more jobs to do than simply making sounds louder, and both drums and other percussion instruments have to be recorded properly, just like any other instruments.

Drums and live audiences

Drum sets often have microphones placed around them for live rock performances. Volume is one important reason for **amplifying** drums. For very large-scale events, such as stadium performances or festivals, the sound of a single unamplified drum set will not carry very far. This is especially true of outdoor performances, where unamplified sound disappears quickly. In the case of hand drums, such as the conga and djembe, or hand percussion, such as shakers, the natural sound of the instrument is much quieter than a drum set played with sticks, so amplification is essential here, too.

A drum set seems loud enough on its own, but it still needs to be amplified.

However, it is also important to mix and balance the sounds of all the instruments in a live band, so that the audience hears a pleasing blend of instrumental sounds. Microphones allow the **sound engineer** at the **mixing board** to produce the best balance of the

A few overhead microphones like this should capture the natural sound of percussion.

various drums and cymbals relative to each other and to the other instruments and voices onstage. The **tone** of the drum sounds can also be altered if necessary. This can be done by using microphones clipped to the drums themselves, or with other microphones that are concealed inside the drums.

Percussion and recording

While classical percussion is not usually amplified, when a classical performance is recorded or broadcast, these instruments must come through with the necessary definition and balance. Since classical recordings usually try to simulate the sound of a concert hall, the percussion section may be recorded with a few overhead microphones to capture the sound of the section as a whole. Sometimes even this much is regarded as intrusive, so the entire recording may be made with only two microphones for the entire orchestra or **ensemble**—percussion and all.

In the case of rock and pop recordings, the story is very different. In an attempt to get a "clean," uniform sound, the drums and any percussion instruments may be recorded with several microphones, often in their own room or even in a different place altogether. Sometimes, parts of the drum set will be recorded first, such as a basic beat on the **snare** and **bass** drums. However, this technique is rarely applied to jazz drumming because of its emphasis on a spontaneous performance.

Innovative Percussion

Perhaps the earliest use of percussion in combination with other technologies was on traditional fairground and cinema organs, where complex mechanical linkages allowed real percussion instruments to be played automatically. Later examples included electronically produced percussion sounds on some types of electric organs.

However, instrument manufacturers then developed electronic triggers that could be mounted under drumlike pads. When these pads were struck, small electric currents could be sent to an electronic "brain" that would generate an appropriate percussion sound. This invention allowed the production of complete electronic drum sets.

MIDI and sampling

With the invention of **MIDI**, a **digital** system that allowed many different types of electronic instruments to communicate with each other, it became possible for electronic drums to produce any number of sounds. This ability was further improved by a process called **sampling** that essentially allowed sounds to be digitally recorded, changed in various ways, and then played back. When this was applied to electronic drums, it allowed drummers to play not only drum and percussion sounds, but almost any other sound as well.

An electronic drum set gives the drummer access to a much wider range of sounds than a traditional drum set does.

One further amusing development was the option to add electronic triggers to ordinary drums. Many drummers found that it was impossible for them to reproduce the carefully crafted and edited sounds of their recordings when they performed live. So they sampled these sounds from their own recordings and then triggered them from their drum sets onstage! This approach has now become widely accepted.

Drum machines

The invention of the drum machine caused controversy. These inexpensive pieces of equipment began as "auto-accompaniment" machines, producing preset **rhythms** that could be used to accompany a performance. Later models had improved sounds and could be programmed to produce the exact drum and percussion parts required for a song.

Drum machines have become instruments in their own right, with many **DJs** and musicians incorporating them into performances.

While there was some concern that drum machines would replace real drummers, there has actually been a resurgence of interest in conventional drums. In fact they are now more popular than ever. Ironically, there are now several "real" drum sets on the market that are designed to imitate the sounds of drum machines.

More new ideas

In the meantime, conventional percussion continues to develop. There are now shell-less drums and timpani (designed for ease of transport), African drums made from **synthetic** materials, and any number of other new ideas that are constantly being added to the resources available to the modern percussionist.

Glossary

amplify to make louder

audible able to be heard

avant-garde modern and experimental

bass lowest range of notes in general use

celeste keyboard instrument inside which hammers strike small metal plates

chamber group small ensemble that plays classical music

choking grasping a percussion instrument after striking it to cut off its sound

chromatically using all the notes and half-notes available, rather than just the notes of one musical key

col legno literally, "with wood"; using the stick of a bow to strike the strings of an orchestral stringed instrument

damping muffling the sound of an instrument with the hand or a piece of other suitable material

digital using a "language" of electronic ones and zeros

DJ performer who plays and mixes music from recordings; short for "disc jockey"

double-headed having both ends covered with a head or membrane, as a drum

ensemble small group of musicians

fiberglass substance made from strands of glass that, when mixed with a resin, forms a hard but lightweight material

fret small strip of metal, wood, or gut on the fingerboard of a stringed instrument, across which the strings are held when changing the notes

friction rubbing of one object against another

genre specific style, as with music or other art forms

gourd rounded plant that can be dried and hollowed out inside

head membrane of skin or synthetic material stretched across the top of a drum

idiophone percussion instrument that produces sound directly, such as a gong or wood block

kazoo instrument that buzzes when a person hums or sings through it; usually a metal or plastic tube with a side hole covered by a thin membrane

lyre harplike stringed instrument with a rectangular frame

melodic relating to melody, or tuneful; when said of a set of drums, it means that the drums can play a recognizable series of notes

membrane thin, pliable sheet of material

membranophone instrument, such as a drum, that makes a sound with a vibrating membrane

MIDI stands for Musical Instrument Digital Interface; a type of computer language that allows some electronic musical instruments to exchange data with computers and with each other

mixing board electronic device that blends the sounds from several microphones and/or instruments

musicologist person who studies aspects of music other than performance or composition, such as its history and cultural role

octave eight tones that make up a musical scale

pick small, flat object used to pluck the strings of certain stringed instruments

pitch highness or lowness of a note

resonant tending to vibrate when a sound is made

resonator hollow object or structure used to amplify the sound of an instrument

rhythm time, pulse, and beat of music

sample short digital sound recording stored in the memory of a computer or electronic instrument

single-headed having only one end covered by a head or membrane, as with a drum

sizzler small device, such as a loose rivet, that can be added to a cymbal to make it produce a sustained hissing sound when struck

snare set of coiled wires stretched across the underside of a drumhead that adds a buzzing effect to the sound of the drum

sound engineer technician who deals with the recording or amplification of music

spherical shaped like a ball or a globe

staves lengths of wood fastened together to make a barrel

synthesize to create something artificially

synthetic created artificially

taper to gradually become thinner or smaller from one end to the other

tenor pitch range that is lower than alto but higher than baritone

tension tightness

thong small, thin leather strap

tone quality of a sound

tremolo rapid variation in the loudness of a sound

West/ern North America and the countries of Europe; of or relating to North America and the countries of Europe

Further Reading

Dearling, Robert. *Non-Western & Obsolete Instruments: Encyclopedia of Musical Instruments.* Broomall, Penn.: Chelsea House Publishers, 2000.

Dearling, Robert. *Percussion & Electronic Instruments: Encyclopedia of Musical Instruments.* Broomall, Penn.: Chelsea House Publishers, 2000.

Rowe, Julian. *Music.* Chicago: Heinemann Library, 1998.

Index